please love me
at my worst

please love me
at my worst

michaela angemeer

Andrews McMeel
PUBLISHING®

for oma and nana

i know that
i am deserving of love

contents

please love my
inner child

inner child

['inər CHīld]

noun

1. a person's childlike aspect characterized by playfulness and creativity
2. often thought of as one's first self, especially when damaged or buried by childhood trauma

give me space
for a second
stop blowing dandelion seeds in my face
i need a field of sunflowers
showing me which way to look
your weeds aren't welcome anymore
i am done facing down
give me something greater than the earth
give me wide-open water
i'm tired of this stream
please let me have the ocean
i need to swim for a while
i need to let the waves carry me
i need salt
i need healing
please just give me this space

i just want to be loved
i just want to be loved
i just want to be loved
i just want to be loved

without condition

the mother i want to be listens
she asks how your day was
but doesn't accept *good* as an answer
she wants to know the ins and outs
she asks about the feelings
she knows you are a wave
that you swell and crash
the mother i want to be listens
without judgment
she validates you
gives advice only when asked
teaches you to trust your instincts
celebrates your life
the mother i want to be tells you

you are enough

when they say they're not trying
to make you feel guilty
it's for their sake, not yours

i am learning that this is not about me
this is about you
i am healed, i am whole
i am enough
you are in pieces
you are broken
you need healing on your own

stop trying to break me too

they told me love is patient
love is kind
but you showed me that
love is harsh
love is negativity
pointing out the bad
love is a sharp tongue
love is bladelike teeth
always cutting
never saying i'm sorry
how does this love
feel like poison in my blood
like i've never known iron
like i've never known oxygen
why did you show this hurt
to such a little girl
her small hands couldn't handle your blade
it ripped her heart open
while you poured the acid
you can keep your attempt at love

i am learning to love on my own

i am

learning

to love

ON MY OWN

i took beatrice to your gravestone
but she didn't know why we stopped there
because you can't explain burial to a dog
so i dug up my missing you
with tears and no shovel
and you gave me a little more
understanding of my mother
when i heard you whisper
she's just tired

i wish you were here
to remind us to love a little more
and judge a little less
cause our brand of love is still *i told you so*
when we could use a little more
i love you no matter what
and i miss stirring gravy
barefoot in the kitchen
and i miss *a little more salt*

but for you i will try
to be a little more sweet
and a little more resistant
when she reinforces my doubts
or pokes holes in my achievements
i just really wish you could meet beatrice

dear nana

if you keep trying to fix other people
it's you that's broken

you don't set boundaries to end a relationship
you set boundaries to continue it

oh gumdrops where have you gone
ice cream eyes i thought you saw more for me
i miss twizzler tongues
and lollipop lips
sweet songs of cinnamon rolls
and cupcake kisses goodnight
jumping jacks on jujubes
and hopscotch topped with butterscotch
glucose, sucrose, fructose, galactose
i'll call you whatever name you'd like
you used to be a friend to me

but candyland is gone

i have always been a little bit weird
a little too fat
a target for bullies
and *you can't play with us*
have you ever overheard
your best friend call you *just a school friend*
or been told you can't play a game
cause you're too big
so instead of talking to friends
you talk to yourself
and your stuffed animals
write on whatever you can find
dance in your room
sing karaoke
make magic by yourself
poor sweet baby you
that little girl just wanted
to be included
to feel loved
to be a part of something

she may not have belonged, but she belongs to me

to my inner child—

i am sorry you never learned
how the words
i love you
were supposed to feel
i am sorry
you were ignored
i am sorry
you were never told

you are enough

today i opened the box of your jewelry
somehow the inside still smells like
chanel number five
it is more than a scent
it is a memory of hugs and kisses on cheeks
endless laughter and spanish that danced in my ears
made me yearn for paella and
the warmth of your backyard swimming pool
i never did ask
why you loved elephants so much
but a long gray trunk still brings a smile
now sometimes a tear
i never did ask
how you loved our family so much
with all of its twisted branches
occasional thorns
you were always the reddest rose
it was the heaviest thing to watch your petals fall
as i write this my tears can't help but pour
because the holidays are so much harder
when you're not here

dear nana II

i didn't say *happy birthday*
for the first time
in twenty-seven years
i cried for three days instead
how do you draw boundaries
when your inner child just wants closeness
how do you cut off someone who hurts you
when you just want to love her

i really do miss you
i wish you understood me
i hope you take some time
to learn about healing
i hope you take some time
to learn how to love yourself

meet me in the backyard
with a kiddie pool
i just want to splash around
like i'm seven
call up the neighbors
let's make new friends
run through sprinklers
throw water balloons
(i'll miss)
let's laugh real loud
scream for fun
eat watermelon and orange slices
remind each other to reapply sunscreen
forget what we were supposed to do today
forget what we were supposed to do this week
call in sick for work
no—quit our jobs
break our leases
move to the forest
bathe in the river
fall asleep on the grass

let's quit adulthood

please love me
at my worst

worst

[wərst]

noun

1. the most serious or unpleasant thing that
   could happen
2. bad: of the lowest quality, most unsuitable, faulty,
   or unattractive
3. at your worst: the least likeable side of someone's
   character

i am still in love with
everyone i've ever been in love with

i just wanna wax your eyebrows
talk about shrek the musical
make out on a picnic blanket
just first base shit
i'll get grass in my hair
you'll pick it out

i just wanna make you a cake
cause it's monday
paint your nails black
tell you secrets
that i don't need to keep anymore

i just wanna do fun shit
roll down a hill
cry laughing
you'll get grass in your hair
i'll pick it out

i just wanna kiss you
or anybody
but mainly you
trace your lip lines with my finger
use lots of tongue
but not too sloppy
ok, kinda sloppy

would you hold my hand
even if it's sweaty
would you say you missed me
even if you didn't

can you miss someone you never really knew

i'm just trying to mind my business
why you gotta smell so good

i'm just trying to mind my business
why you gotta stretch like that

i'm just trying to mind my business
why you gotta smile at me

i'm just trying to mind my business
why are your teeth so nice

i'm just trying to mind my business
why are your lips so nice

i'm just trying to mind my business
why you gotta make me fall in love with you again

when will
i stop falling in love
with the idea of a person

when you ask
what i'm looking for

i know you're not looking for anything serious

i am done with dating
i am too intense for
just drinks or a coffee
i fall in love either immediately or never
i am a stay-up-till-three-am girl
talk-all-night girl
tell-me-all-your-secrets girl
i know we just met
but we might as well get married

it was less i was in love with you
and more you made me feel like
i was standing on stable ground for once

i love the smell of
parking garages
home depot
bleached white sheets
powder laundry detergent
cucumber deodorant
and melrose place

i love the smell of
roasted coffee beans
the top of bea's head
does hollandaise have a smell
if it does i love it too

i love the smell of
barbecued sausages
lake air
spruce trees
oatmeal chocolate chip cookies
or maybe i just love eating them

i love the smell of
october
rain before
the worms crawl out
you before
you were with her

someone, anyone
please tell me
why can't i kick the feeling

that we were supposed to be together

who would
i be if
i had never
been loved
by you

sometimes i wonder
what life would be like
if we had never met
if we never collided in this lifetime
or learned what the curve
of each other's faces felt like
who would i be if i had never held your hand

who would i be if i had never been loved by you

i miss the feeling of trust
with eyes closed
no fear of falling
i miss floating with you
weightlessness
no doubt in forever

no doubt in us

i know you loved me
but i wasn't what you wanted
i know you loved me
but you chose her instead

loving you is like drinking diet coke
on an empty stomach
i can feel you burning up inside of me

but i'm just happy to feel something

baby, i fall so easily
you don't even have
to try with me
i trip over words
like beautiful and amazing
any kind of kindness
makes my knees weak
for at least a week
i could slip over
prolonged eye contact
or a nice smile
baby, you've got to know
you have me but
i am yours to lose

all we're doing is exchanging words
so how have you already

put my heart in my throat

you make me feel like
you can see my insides
but you are not a mind reader

and neither am i

i know it sounds ridiculous
but your hair flops different now
and i can tell she bought you
new bodywash

i know it sounds ridiculous
but sometimes i think about the
alternate universe
where we ended up together
and i still can't get you to go to therapy

i didn't know at first
but then in a full room
you looked at me to see
if i was laughing

i didn't know at first
but then my cheeks
kept hurting
from smiling at you

i didn't know at first
but then your eyes
seeped past my eyeline
made their way into my soul

i didn't know at first
but then i knew
that this was me
falling in love with you

how was i supposed to know
that we wouldn't end up together
how was i supposed to know
that i would end up alone

i tried to teach you
how to love me
but the love i needed
would have come naturally

you were the last time i was in love with anyone

i had a good trajectory
arms open wide
heart open even wider
but you broke off my limbs
severed my aorta
all that was left was
spilled blood
and all i could do to
stay alive
was burn my heart closed
until it cauterized

saying i have trust issues
would imply i have any trust left

i just have issues

i don't know why i keep
giving people
pieces of myself
it's like i have a resistance to wholeness
more comfort in being broken

all i did was love you as much
as a damaged heart could
all you did was make it worse

what do you do when
you choose someone and
they do not choose you back

be gentle
i am what's left of a glass house
too many stones have been thrown in
my shards are sharp
but if you move slow
i promise they will dull
be patient
there is a door for you to open
it's just a little hidden
but if you make it through
i will gladly hand over the key
be kind
even though my words are harsh
i rarely mean it
my teeth are serrated
but if you don't bite back
my tongue will learn to love you

instructions on loving me

i love you more
than anything i've ever felt

i love you more than all of me

let's take a walk in the cemetery
i just wanna know if you would die for me

quarantine heart
why won't you leave me alone
stop beating
for the ones you used to beat for
they are not here

all there is to love is me

if you wanted to be with me
you would be here already

get out of my car
i screamed
i do not trust you to love me

the way i deserve to be loved

you keep trying to summon me
but i'm digging in my heels
i have learned the lesson of you already
stop trying to teach me again

I HAVE LEARNED THE LESSON OF YOU ALREADY

some people don't even
have to die to haunt you

ghosts

they
always come
back when you
learn to stop needing them

could you come back please
and just love me a little while longer
i don't need much
just give my hand a squeeze
kiss my forehead
could you please come back
just for a second
just love me in this instance
i just want to remember a little better
i just want to make sure i don't forget

i wish i could clean up
the mess that i made of myself
pack it up in boxes
drop it off at the thrift store
fill garbage bags
with my self-criticism
rent a dumpster to toss out
the insults i throw at myself
have a trash fire kindled with
unrequited love and all the
longing i do that lasts for too long
is it thursday already
don't let the garbage truck leave
i'm not finished yet
i just need a little more time
to get this mess cleaned up

i'm sorry i don't have anything left in me
i'm sorry all of me wasn't enough for you

why was i born
with the feeling unworthy gene
like my blessings are undeserved
like my accomplishments are accidents

why can't i just feel good
about the good things
not ruin them with heart beating faster
my own anxious drum
pounding erratically

does anyone want to trade brains
i'd like a quieter one
does anyone want to trade me for sad
i'd like happy instead

why do i keep falling in love
with temporary people

baby, it turns out
he's not coming back

he was never going to

teach me how to love
with arms wide open
my limbs seem to be
permanently crossed
i'm stuck here
unclench my fists
kiss my palms
and tell them
all my wars have already
been fought
and the cavalry isn't coming back
remind me about the sun
make me look up
instead of down
wish on my teardrops
until they become moonlight
i promise they'll become moonlight
please don't give up on me

please love me at my worst

how can i love myself
if i don't know who i am

please love me
for who i am

who i am

[ho͞o ˈi ˈāem]

phrase

1. a state of being, to be oneself
2. the true essence of a person without embellishment
3. one of life's greatest quandaries when posed
    as a question: who am i?

you cannot use someone
else's map
to find yourself

i am resistant to change
i'd rather eat ice
and cry on an airplane

i am fifty shades of who i once was
always black lace underwear
i am low-cut tops
and no bras with bodysuits
i am bare butt on the beach
i am toes curled and painted pink
i am nails long with little white clouds
i am peaches tattooed on my shoulder
i am soft
i am dark
i am mad
and i am wild

you are allowed to be
brutally confronted by loneliness

i pluck one gray hair every day
throw it in the sink
it disappears like its job is done
taunting me since twenty-two
i put sunscreen on my face
every morning
eye cream on my face
every night

hangovers feel different
at twenty-seven
a drunk friday
equals still tired on sunday
my body aches harder now
and i can't stay awake for
more than fifteen hours
without an iced coffee or two

i thought i was eternal youth
drinking from the fountain
turns out aging is
the only thing i can't
run away from
and i don't know
what i'm meant to be
if i'm not meant to be young

i'm drinking cold coffee
with cold feet
my brain is numb
because i forgot to sleep
and though i never liked
touching people
i'd give my right arm to
hold your hand
can someone please
breathe on me again

can someone please love me again

can someone
please love
me again

we don't talk about friendship
breakups enough
they're less concrete
less definite
less written in ink
sometimes you just drift away
there's no fight
no closure
no real ending

all you get is an ellipsis

if i had a fairy godmother
i'd ask her to make me
less judgmental

i'm sorry my legs are prickly
my toenails yellowed
nails thin and short
i'm sorry there's a reoccurring pimple
under my right nostril
and two bright red beacons lining my jaw
i'm sorry there's a bug bite on my heel
my lips are chapped
and skin is dry
i'm sorry to no one
i'm sorry to everyone
but most of all
i'm sorry to me
for constantly cataloging
my imperfections

why is making decisions so difficult
i thought by now i would have this down
but left and right always seem to have
the same pros and cons
and i pick neither
i can never choose staying or going
so i end up in limbo
if letting go is a choice
i always run toward it
but get held back
by wanting to hold on
how will i ever move forward
if i feel so comfortable in the in-between
how will i grow
if i never take a leap

the fool

i wish i was a little less virgo moon
a little more gemini rising
i don't mind being a scorpio sun
but i wish it hurt less to be vulnerable
and that my cancer mars at twenty-six degrees
made me less likely to be angry
but not talk about it
then blame myself
i wish my mercury in sagittarius
would stop saying things
that are rude but true
and i would happily swap my venus in capricorn
for taurus or anything a little less analytical
i wish my pisces midheaven
had a little more self-resolve
and my chiron in leo
didn't try to sabotage my success
all i'm asking is to switch some signs
shift the sky

i just need a little change

today i love me
more than i loved you
and that's all i can ask of myself

i keep waiting for my coming of age
but if i wait it will never come
so i will sit here
i will float
i will write about my body
the way it doesn't fit quite right in this bathtub
the way it doesn't fit quite right in this bra
the way it doesn't fit quite right in this dress
until i realize it's not me
it's the bathtub
it's not me
it's the bra
it's not me
it's the dress
and i am becoming
my coming of age
in this very moment

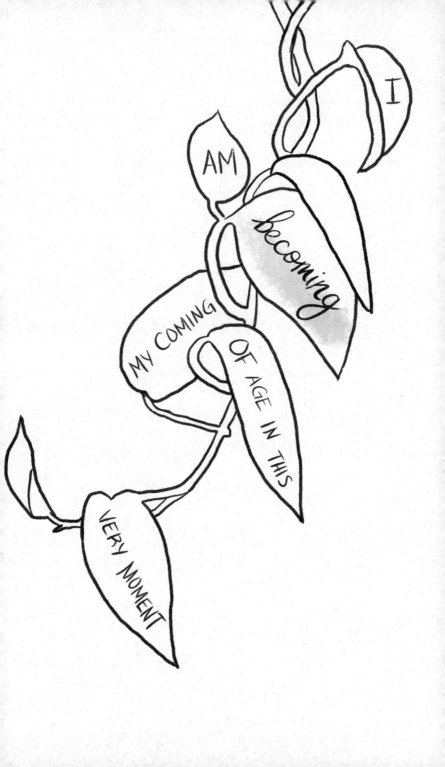

you are the only person
who can put yourself first

therapy lessons part III

even though it's over
and i think i learned my lesson
i'm grateful to have been loved by you

remember,
you are like the moon
you can choose how
where and when
you reveal yourself

hello, i think some girls are pretty, but doesn't everyone?
hello, i can't stop thinking about that girl's eyelashes
hello, is your roommate gonna be there? no reason, just wondering
hello, hasn't everyone drunkenly kissed a girl?
hello, did you know tove lo is bi? just thought it was interesting
hello, you can't deny that monopoly is a catchy song
hello, ya i went to see betty who twice by myself
hello, i'm just an ally
hello, i might be bicurious
hello, i'm probably more than curious

hello, i'm bi, nice to meet you

cheers to the bisexuals
the lesbians, gays, and queers
cheers if you like to be called all three
cheers to the trans folks
to marsha p. johnson and sylvia rivera
thank you for letting me be here
cheers to the two-spirit
to the nonbinary
the questioning
the not sure yet
cheers to the allies
cheers to everyone who did work
so i could fully be me

sexual experiences don't have to define your sexuality

how do i know if a girl likes women
i'm looking for rainbows
maybe a phone case
or key chain
is that an equal sign tattoo
was that just a friendly smile
or something more
was that just a friendly message
or something more
do i need to buy a pair of vans
or cuff my jeans
can somebody help me over here

how do i know if a girl likes me

let's talk about the karens
i'm sorry fellow white women
but *we don't claim her*
isn't going to get rid of her
let us claim the karens as our own
examine the illness of our whiteness
that they scream so clearly
don't hide from it
let us recognize the karen in ourselves
don't slip up now
what have we learned this week
karen is obvious white supremacy
but what about the things we do
have we ever been the only white person in a room
have we taken part in creating entirely
w h i t e s p a c e s
i'm in this with you
it's time to make sure that
the next time our karen tries to come out
we've done enough work to muzzle her

white man
why don't you wanna fight, man
don't know what anti-racism means
cause books are too long
and social media makes you tired

white man
why don't you pay attention
spend more time coordinating
fantasy football than
calling out your racist friends

white man
why are you oblivious
more upset about your team losing
and your scratched bumper
than police brutality

white man
why aren't you listening?
can name every part of your car's engine
but have no interest in naming
the institutions that uphold white supremacy

white man
we need you to fight
we need you to pay attention
white man—
you're missing the revolution

i don't want a past love
i don't want a baby boy
needs to be reminded about their mom's birthday
or when to reapply sunscreen
i don't want to tell them to do the dishes
or groan when they forget
what i asked them
three times
i want self-sufficiency
reliability
don't tell me twice
i want no nagging
i want thoughtfulness
i want doing things because they get it
i want doing things because they remember
all baby boys are meant to be with someone
but i really hope one is not meant for me

i tell the sun i love her
and in return
she gives me freckles under my eyes
tans my shoulders
streaks my hair
warms my chest
tells my soul that life is still worth living

i keep shouting *who am i*
into the void
the echo screams back

whoever you want to be

i am happy and i am sad
i am lonely
i am alive
and i am me

please love who
i'm becoming

becoming

[bi-ˈkə-miŋ]

noun

1. to become or grow to be
2. a process of change involving the realization of potential; a movement from a lower level of potentiality to a higher level of actuality

i am tired of writing
sad lonely poems
imagine i wrote about you
before i met you
tall strong hands thick neck
or short and soft long eyelashes
this isn't a poem
this is a wish
a wish for someone better than before
a want-to-hold-you-now
a wish-you-were-here-already

love is sharing a banana split. and letting you have the last spring roll. it's reminding me that i need to wake up early tomorrow. and staying up until i fall asleep. love is driving me to the airport. bringing takeout when you pick me up. love is grabbing your hand on a roller coaster. or during a scary movie. love is asking if you need a jacket. it's feeling sad for me when i'm sad. love is knowing your favorite pizza toppings. love is surprise notes. love is being honest. love is showing up. love is all of it.

love is
all of it

darling, i'm not interested
in flowers or lust
offer me a bouquet
of empathy and trust

here i am
simultaneously
all that i've ever been
and everything i could become

and when the shore
seems out of reach
don't forget that

you can always just float for a while

give me rippling lakes
and a deck hot on the soles of my feet
give me black iron armrests that sear my elbows
a cloudless sky that turns my nose pink
the way air moves differently near water
chipmunks all named chippy
an otter that lives under the dock
and a loon that coos to the sound of the wind

i am ready to breathe for once

every
night the moon
sings me the same song

there is room for softness here

my kind of love goes deep
but it has boundaries

love me by giving me space

stop making
choices that prioritize
other people over yourself

if you have a body that wants to be seen
don't you dare let anyone tell you to cover it up

you deserve to be loved without condition. you are enough. without trying harder. without learning new things. without accomplishments. without success. without getting bigger or smaller. without getting smarter. without improvements. without changing anything at all. you are enough, just as you are.

i just want to be in love with somebody
who wants to be in love with me

i wish i could skip forward
at least four years
i just want to get to the good parts
i wish i could blink
and be in love with you
whoever you are
i just want my simple future love
all i'm looking for is happy
why do i have to go through
all of this growing first

why do i have to find myself before i find you

look at this body
look how she lets you breathe
a belly filled with air is healing
an exhale is surrender
look at how she lets you move
hips following rhythm
feet dancing through sunlight
look at her glow
look at what she's done for you
tell her you love her
tell her it's not about what meets the eye

it's how she makes you feel

loving your body
is a small revolution

ignore anyone who tells you to change it

and just like the full moon
you can release
you can let go

and make room for something new

baby, you will find someone
the right one, someday
but for now, take this time as a gift

learn how to love yourself

what i'm learning is that
i can control no one
but i can set intentions
ask for healing
bring love to the center
i can tell myself

i have been worthy all along

you are everything you were ever meant to be. don't forget to celebrate yourself. celebrate who you are and your potential of becoming. dance in your kitchen and use a pen as a microphone. run outside and spin around in the rain. sing as loud as you can in your car. ask your inner child what they want, and give it to them. you owe it to yourself to live this life in your wild. you owe it to yourself to find out who you are.

my final words to you, dear reader

acknowledgments

to my readers, thank you for being right by my side on this journey. i can't believe we made it to book three! thank you for your commiseration, your stories, and your words of encouragement. you really make me feel so loved. to my dad, thank you for being my number one supporter and maybe the only one more excited than me over the past four years. to my oma, thank you for giving me twenty-eight years of wisdom and showing me the importance of enjoying your own company. to nana, thank you for watching over me, for showing up in elephants and butterflies and always reminding me that even though you aren't here, you are with me. to chinye, thank you for being my confidant, the brightest light in the dark spots. to my agent, james, thank you for finding me in a corner of the internet and believing in my potential as an author. and to all the wonderful people at andrews mcmeel publishing, thank you for taking a chance on me and making my dreams come true.

about the author

michaela angemeer is a canadian poet who grew up
in brampton, ontario. she went to the university of waterloo,
receiving her bachelor of arts in psychology and english in 2015.

after sharing her poetry on instagram for a year, she self-published
her first collection of poetry, *when he leaves you,* in 2018. the
book debuted as the #1 new release in canadian poetry online. her
second book, *you'll come back to yourself,* a collection of poetry
inspired by modern dating, was released in 2019, making it to
the #1 bestseller in poetry the following year. her third collection,
please love me at my worst, is inspired by loneliness, unrequited
love, and not being able to let go of past relationships. it has
themes of connecting with your inner child, loving the worst parts
of yourself, coming out as bisexual, and focusing on self-growth.

michaela now lives in kitchener, ontario, with her frenchton,
beatrice, a lot of books, and too many plants.

find her online:
michaelapoetry.com
@michaelapoetry

Andrews McMeel Publishing
a division of Andrews McMeel Universal
1130 Walnut Street, Kansas City, Missouri 64106

www.andrewsmcmeel.com

23 24 25 26 27 TEN 10 9 8 7 6

ISBN: 978-1-5248-6869-7

Library of Congress Control Number: 2021940034

Editor: Patty Rice
Art Director: Holly Swayne
Artwork: Michaela Angemeer
Production Editor: Margaret Daniels
Production Manager: Carol Coe

attention: schools and businesses
Andrews McMeel books are available at quantity discounts with
bulk purchase for educational, business, or sales promotional use.
For information, please e-mail the Andrews McMeel Publishing
Special Sales Department: sales@amuniversal.com.